Poems From Northern England

Edited by Claire Tupholme

First published in Great Britain in 2007 by:
Young Writers
Remus House
Coltsfoot Drive
Peterborough
PE2 9JX
Telephone: 01733 890066
Website: www.youngwriters.co.uk

SB ISBN 978-1 84602 908 2

Foreword

Young Writers was established in 1991 and has been passionately devoted to the promotion of reading and writing in children and young adults ever since. The quest continues today. Young Writers remains as committed to the nurturing of poetic and literary talent as ever.

This year's Young Writers competition has proven as vibrant and dynamic as ever and we are delighted to present a showcase of the best poetry from across the UK and in some cases overseas. Each poem has been selected from a wealth of *Little Laureates* entries before ultimately being published in this, our sixteenth primary school poetry series.

Once again, we have been supremely impressed by the overall quality of the entries we have received. The imagination, energy and creativity which has gone into each young writer's entry made choosing the poems a challenging and often difficult but ultimately hugely rewarding task - the general high standard of the work submitted ensured this opportunity to bring their poetry to a larger appreciative audience.

We sincerely hope you are pleased with this final collection and that you will enjoy *Little Laureates Poems From Northern England* for many years to come.

Contents

Etherley Lane CP School, Bishop Auckland

Greenfield St Mary's Primary School, Oldham

The Poems

Our School Star

Colourful and shining
Large and clear
Lots of atmosphere in the hall

Teachers are good
Children are great
Apart from evil Mr Redcliffe with his hook

The hall is busy
Everyone listen
It's time for a bit of fun

Everyone looks great
Apart from the hall
Decorate time

Hooray!

Tinkerbell is shining
Like a little star
Here come Mrs Pierce twinkling down the hall

Small and nice
As quiet as a mouse
Walking to the front
She always looks great
She is never, never late
For anything

Everybody is looking
It's the star
It's Mrs Pierce
Like a star!

Eleanor Robertson (9)
Ansdell Primary School, Lytham St Annes

The Colourful Days

Bright colours everywhere
Under your nose, under your feet
White, clean waterfalls
Tall, peaceful buildings
Peaceful, children calling
Beautiful, quiet meadows
Chattering people talking
Sunny, orange sun raining light all over you
The colourful days are to stay

But . . .

The dull days sometimes happen
Dull greyness everywhere
Under your nose, under your feet
Dirty, black mud
Small, unhygienic buildings
Unhappy children punching each other
Messy, weeded meadows
Shouting people falling out
Raining, dirty rain pouring on your head
The dull days are to go away

Dull days are horrible and mean
The colourful days must stay

So the days may be dull and grey or bright and colourful
But that's how life is
And that's here to stay.

Lara Pownall (9)
Ansdell Primary School, Lytham St Annes

Shopping

Shopping, shopping in a mall,
Outside children playing with a ball.
Red or green top,
On a rusty stand next to a mop.
I'll have both I think,
But what's that? Here it's pink.

Oh no, I'm in a mess,
So much more distress.
Men and boys have no clue at all,
Shopping in a mall.

Then, I see a sale sign over there,
I rush right over to see what is there.
It's a great shop here,
Right next to the pier.
Trousers, trousers everywhere,
Here and there.

Now, hats are a different story,
So I won't tell you about hat glory.

Oh no, I'm in a mess,
So much distress.
Men have no clue at all,
Shopping in a mall.

Kirsty Pownall (9)
Ansdell Primary School, Lytham St Annes

Seasons

Spring is coming,
Colourful and bright,
Roses and lilies bring the light.

Summer is coming,
Warm and gentle,
The frog's mum has gone mental.

Autumn is coming,
Leaves are falling - orange, red and brown,
Blowing all around the town.

Winter is coming,
Snowflakes are delicate, icy and cold,
By the time it's summer, I will be old.

Amy Wallbank (9)
Ansdell Primary School, Lytham St Annes

A Weird Poem

Fire, fire, fire in a house,
Look, look at that woodlouse.

Water, water running in a bath,
Ha, ha, look at that person laugh.

Hear, hear how that bird sings,
And look, look at its silver wings.

Run, run, running is really fun,
Eat, eat, eat that hot cross bun.

Bye, bye, that's all from me for now,
But I will not go without a bow.

Andrew Garside (9)
Ansdell Primary School, Lytham St Annes

Sport

Sport is good,
It keeps you fit,
If you do it a lot,
You'll get fit.

Don't sit in the armchair being lazy,
Get up and do some sport,
Don't lie in bed snoring and sleeping,
Get up and do some sport!

Sport is good,
It keeps you fit,
If you do it a lot,
You'll get fit.

Don't sit at the table eating junk food,
Get up and do some sport,
Don't sit on the couch watching TV,
Get up and do some sport!

Adam Lanigan (9)
Ansdell Primary School, Lytham St Annes

Footie Fiend

Yes, George Best liked footie a lot,
Sometimes he went over the top,
Then something went horribly bad,
Next thing you know everyone is sad,
Because he died of liver cancer.

Tynan Baker (9)
Ansdell Primary School, Lytham St Annes

Shopping

I like shopping all around,
Sometimes inside or in the town,
People laughing at the clown,
Not a single peep or frown.

I bought this, I bought that,
I don't know for sure what I had.
I had too much, I had too little,
I don't know for sure what I had.

Harleigh Tanner (9)
Ansdell Primary School, Lytham St Annes

A Whirlwind Poem

I am a book,
Just take a look,
I may be small,
But sometimes tall,
If you want it give us a call,
Look inside, can you see
A hamster drinking a cup of tea?
Yes, that's quite odd,
It's like a bee in a pod,
So take a look at me.

Bethany Kerr (9)
Ansdell Primary School, Lytham St Annes

I Am . . .

I am a child,
Small and loud.
I am an adult,
Big and proud.
I am a grandparent,
Old and bold.
I am a king,
Happy and snappy.
I am a queen,
Mean and sly.
That is the end,
For you and I.

Alexander Stanier (9)
Ansdell Primary School, Lytham St Annes

I See A Bully

I see a bully
Walking to school,
They are mean
And a fool.
You must tell someone,
Tell the teacher,
Tell a friend,
Tell your parents,
But don't suffer in silence!

Jessica Slater (9)
Ansdell Primary School, Lytham St Annes

Bullying's Bad!

Bullying's bad,
It makes people sad,
They don't want to go to school,
They just want to stay in their room,
They go to school a misery,
They're being bullied physically,
They tell a teacher,
It's sorted out,
So tell somebody without a doubt.

Lewis Jones (9)
Ansdell Primary School, Lytham St Annes

Bullying

B is for bad bully
U is for unfair play
L is for land destroyer
L is for lazy learner
Y is for youth puncher
I is for insect squasher
N is for naughty player
G is for girl kicker.

Sam Proctor (9)
Ansdell Primary School, Lytham St Annes

Jungle Life

In the jungle, the elephants groan
The baby cub is all alone,
The animals are all feared,
For the poachers have neared,
But then they have come to find a special bone

They set their camp,
The floor is damp,
All the animals sleep outside,
Some of them hide,
They all sleep like a tramp!

Barnaby Pearson (9)
Ansdell Primary School, Lytham St Annes

Character Book Day

Captain Hook, a character from a famous book.
In the hall we could see,
Lots of characters, worth a look.
All the teachers were pirates fierce,
Until Tinkerbell appeared,
Oh, it's Mrs Pierce!

George Fox (9)
Ansdell Primary School, Lytham St Annes

Happiness

Happiness tastes like there's peace in your mouth,
Like unicorns, rainbows and leprechauns as well.
Happiness smells like there are millions of friends,
All playing together in everyone's dens.
Happiness sounds like there's talking and laughter,
All playing and making everyone sillier.
Happiness looks like people getting on,
Making new friends as we go along.
Happiness feels so soft and sweet,
Like a pillow being a seat.

Lucy Hall (8)
Ansdell Primary School, Lytham St Annes

Peace

Peace is as white as a dove
Flying through the midnight sky.
Peace feels like I am floating in the air
Through the stars and past the sparkling moon.
Peace tastes like sweet, curly candyfloss
Swooping and washing down my throat.
Peace smells like lavender, calm and still
Making lots of honey for hungry bees.
Peace is like angels singing a lullaby
So we can go to sleep.

Kelsey Horridge (7)
Ansdell Primary School, Lytham St Annes

Feelings

When I am happy,
I sing and dance,
Eat and drink,
Read and need,
Laugh and be daft!

When I am sad,
I kick and hit,
Pinch and bite,
Be silly and rough,
Break friends and hate my teachers!

Cara Townsend (7)
Ansdell Primary School, Lytham St Annes

Peace

Peace is blue like an evening sea
Slowly rushing onto the shore.
Peace sounds like the wind
Blowing away the leaves of the trees.
Peace smells like air
Drifting around the Earth.
Peace tastes like a cold box of biscuits.

Amber Marikar (7)
Ansdell Primary School, Lytham St Annes

Death

Death is dark and rude to kill the one victim.
Death sounds like the black bullet of a gun
Heading straight for your friend.
Death smells like mouldy shepherd's pie
Being left out in the blazing sun.
Death tastes like painted biscuits
With the bitter taste of paint.
Death feels like heartburn
Killing you any minute now.
Death is nothing to be proud of.
Death is awful!
Take no notice of it.

Anthony Ford (7)
Ansdell Primary School, Lytham St Annes

Happy

Happy looks like
Roses growing in the garden.

Happy smells like
Love and peace in the air.

Happy sounds like
Bees buzzing on a summer's day.

Happy tastes like
Sweet honey, freshly made.

Happy feels like
Dancing in a flowery meadow.

Siân Thompson (7)
Ansdell Primary School, Lytham St Annes

When I Am Happy

When I am happy
I start screaming with happiness,
After that I start running around
And that makes me dizzy
And I feel like a merry-go-round,
Then I nearly explode
And there is always fun to be had.

Laura Perrin (7)
Ansdell Primary School, Lytham St Annes

When I Am Excited

When I'm excited,
I jump up and down,
Run around,
Smile a lot
And then I explode
With laughter,
Smiling so much,
Makes me stay put,
Happiness falls around me
Wherever I am,
Always excited
With fun and lots to be done.

Georgina Hutt (7)
Ansdell Primary School, Lytham St Annes

Peace

Peace is nice and quiet
Like the blue sky in the air.
Peace sounds like dry raindrops
Falling from the rooftops.
Peace smells like small drops
Of snow from the air.
Peace tastes like a cold strawberry ice cream.

Emma Mayor (7)
Ansdell Primary School, Lytham St Annes

Excited

When I'm excited I:
Jump up and down,
Go round and round,
Explode and pound,
Roll and kick
And nearly be sick.

After I've been to this exciting place I:
Sit down and sleep,
I don't leap or pound
And I don't make a sound.

Bethany Marshall (8)
Ansdell Primary School, Lytham St Annes

Happy

Happy looks like pretty flowers,
In spring and summer.

Happy feels like the sea,
Flowing across your body.

Happy smells like tropical fruits,
On a beautiful beach.

Happy sounds like people,
Playing and laughing.

Happy tastes like chocolate,
Melting through my mouth.

Alex Pennycook (8)
Ansdell Primary School, Lytham St Annes

Feelings

Hate is like a black night
Filled with nothing but hate.

Hate feels like lava stone
Just heating up to blow out.

Hate tastes like a burned piece
Of popcorn.

Hate looks like a volcano
About to erupt.

Hate smells like a burning fire
Destroying everything in its path.

Alex Iredale (8)
Ansdell Primary School, Lytham St Annes

Happy

When I am happy I go and play
When I am happy I play with my brother
When I am happy I hug my mum
When I am happy I jump
When I am happy I close my eyes
And I cannot wait for tomorrow.

Laurence Joyner (8)
Ansdell Primary School, Lytham St Annes

The Bully

My skin is brown.
My freckles, all over.
My life, a misery.
At quarter past twelve
I go and hide in the boys' toilet.
The bully finds me anyway.
The chant spreads on,
That I am stupid.
I fear school,
I fear life.
I cannot tell him off.
I'm punched
And a hand in my face.
My mum and dad are worried.
My glasses are snapped in half.
My former name is a shame.
My life has let me down.
My face will form a frown.

Christopher Eaves (8)
Ansdell Primary School, Lytham St Annes

Wars

I just can't stop crying
Because people are dying.
Fire burning,
Bombs blowing,
Letters coming,
Dark sky,
People dying,
I just can't stop crying
Because people are dying.
Guns shooting,
Sad injuries,
Helicopters flying,
Tanks firing,
Dead bodies,
Torched people,
I just can't stop crying
Because people are dying.

I hate war.

Laura Faulkner & Georgia Bridge (8)
Ansdell Primary School, Lytham St Annes

The Bully

He called me names and I was scared,
He punched me and I was frightened,
He kicked me and I was upset,
He was rude and I was cross,
He swore and I was angry,
He stole my friend and I was alone,
He ganged up on me and I was sad,
He was mean and I didn't want to play outside,
He picked on me and I didn't want to go to school.
I told someone,
It got sorted,
I wasn't being bullied,
We played nicely together.

Iona Flegg (8)
Ansdell Primary School, Lytham St Annes

When I Am Lonely

I sit down quietly
And I cry
Sometimes I just stand
And wait for them to dry.

I run upstairs
And hide under the quilt
I fall asleep
Lying in a tilt.

In a few minutes I wake up
I feel better
When Mum brings me
Orange juice in a cup.

India Morgan (8)
Ansdell Primary School, Lytham St Annes

Peace

Peace is blue, like water drifting over and through the ocean.
Peace sounds like a cute little butterfly flying across fields.
Peace smells like perfume floating over the world.
Peace tastes like ice cream melting in your mouth.
Peace feels like a ladybird climbing up a tree.
Peace is beautiful.

Adam Wilson (8)
Ansdell Primary School, Lytham St Annes

School

The weekend is over, it's Monday again
I want to go home and sleep in my den
We get up so early and work so hard
They give us homework when we want to rest
Soon after, it's time for some tests
Who invented school? We'll never know
I wish I could go back in time and see who it was
For this is something we all want to know!

Jodie Ferguson (11)
Ansdell Primary School, Lytham St Annes

Hide-And-Seek

In the cupboard,
Under the stairs,
In the bathroom,
Or behind a chair.

Behind a curtain,
Up a tree,
I am so clever,
You can't find me.

You have to hide,
Before they count,
Because if they find you,
Then you are *out!*

Jack Bainbridge (11)
Ansdell Primary School, Lytham St Annes

Birthdays

Birthdays, birthdays, birthdays,
What fun they bring.
Wrapping presents, writing cards,
'Happy birthday!' they sing.

Going to bed as seven,
Waking up as eight.
Personally myself, I think,
Birthdays are so great!

Sending invitations
Out to all my friends.
'Come to my party,
The fun will never end'.

Birthdays, birthdays, birthdays,
What fun they bring.
Wrapping presents, writing cards,
'Happy birthday!' they sing.

Taylor McFarlane (11)
Ansdell Primary School, Lytham St Annes

Questions Of Christmas Time

Why is Christmas in winter when it is
Cold, wet, windy,
Icy, frosty, snowy
And such bad weather?

When people want to enjoy themselves
And be happy, delighted, excited
And more!

Why is it only once a year?
And who made up Santa, Rudolph,
Christmas trees, snowmen and more?

These things we will never know!

Kirsty Fraser (11)
Ansdell Primary School, Lytham St Annes

The Twin Towers

The plane crashed,
On this very sad day,
Millions died by terrorism,
Why, why did they do it?

It smelt like death,
It looked like death,
It sounded like death,
And all around, it felt like death.

Stephen Oberman (11)
Ansdell Primary School, Lytham St Annes

Hedgehogs

Hedgehogs small, none tall
Static and spiky
We just love them all
Habitats narrow, in the bushes
Tiny and slow
Never in rushes.

Jessica Holroyd (11)
Ansdell Primary School, Lytham St Annes

Lonely

Same thing day and night,
All they seem to do is fight.

I feel lonely, my soul is empty,
Broken and bare.

They never stop to think about the pain
And what I am going through.
But all I really care about now is you.

Libby Winfield (11)
Ansdell Primary School, Lytham St Annes

My Friend

My friend is like a comfy chair,
And my best teddy bear.
She smells like lilies
And is really silly.
She's really funny
And like a cuddly bunny.

Ruth Edwards (11)
Ansdell Primary School, Lytham St Annes

Changes

Somehow the world seems sadder
When a funeral comes to town.
The glow on your face stops shining
And you start to get a distraught tear from your eye.
A ball of shame runs down your cheek
As you stand underneath the willow tree
Where your friend will never be.
But now I have to leave my friend,
Bonjour, or maybe bye,
You will always be in my mind,
Guess this is goodbye.

Meghan Swarbrick (11)
Ansdell Primary School, Lytham St Annes

What God Could Have Done

The world has so much it could give,
From a flying elephant to a swimming pig,
Singing hedgehogs, dancing mice,
Or maybe a tiger, that would be nice.
A wussy lion, nice smelling socks,
Jumping snails, self-moving clocks,
A skipping kangaroo or a talking dog,
Clever teddy, non-rolling log.
Just between me and you,
We could even have non-sticking glue.
It's strange to think what we could have,
If God had done what He could have!

Fraser Flegg (11)
Ansdell Primary School, Lytham St Annes

London

London is a place of crime
You can hear the babies whine
Sleeping through the night
Hoping you'll be alright
All the phones are bust
Like chewing gum in the dust
London is a bad, bad place.

Zachary Almond (11)
Ansdell Primary School, Lytham St Annes

Litter

When I see people
Dropping litter
I want to cry
I want to die
I want to hit 'em
I want to kill 'em

But when I see people
Picking it up
It's a whole different story
I want to hug 'em
I want to love 'em
But all I do
In my mind
Is say thank you
Thank you so much!

Philip Banner (10)
Ansdell Primary School, Lytham St Annes

Bullseye

Black and white
Always in a fight
Gets me up in the night
He is such a monkey
But really funky
He loves his walks
And always talks
In a strange little way
But I love him anyway.

Bethany Lee (10)
Ansdell Primary School, Lytham St Annes

Cats

(Inspired by 'Cats Sleep Anywhere' by Eleanor Farjean)

Cats, cats, what wonderful things
They play with toys and heaps of strings

Cats, cats everywhere
On a table or on a chair

Some cats are small, some cats are tall
It doesn't matter, we love them all

Cats, cats walk everywhere
They plod along up the stair

Cats are fantastic leapers
And they're excellent creepers

Cats, cats, what wonderful things
They play with toys and heaps of strings.

Holly Bain (10)
Ansdell Primary School, Lytham St Annes

Why Do Chickens Die?

Why do people think of chickens
As things that don't deserve to live?
They get their necks pulled because
They are thought to be dumb as a sieve

The farmers use them to give them eggs
But when they can't or grow old
They are taken to the shed
Where they are killed and cold

They're mixed with chemicals
And chopped into pieces
They are sold in a shop
Their feathery coats are turned into fleeces

But if I had a chicken
I'd look after it well
I'd keep it alive
Not kill it to sell!

Jonathan Abbott (10)
Ansdell Primary School, Lytham St Annes

Sport

Football is great, football is fun
With people training and having a run.
Professional managers are here to assist
And to check players on a list.

People buy tickets for cricket
And would like to see England get a wicket.
But sometimes you lose a game
And if you got 0, you may get the blame.

Finally, in golf, you need a club,
It might be an iron, it might be a wood.
Golfers play on the green,
But beware, the bunkers might not be seen.

Luke Weafer (10)
Ansdell Primary School, Lytham St Annes

Football

G ood teamwork wins the game
O wn goals are not the same
A player might have fame
L osing is not the same
S o football is a good game.

Ellis Glover (9)
Ansdell Primary School, Lytham St Annes

A Moment

Flowers grow all around,
Through the fields they grow up and down.
First they start as a little seed,
Lying in the dark waiting for a feed.
Then, along comes the rain,
The flowers begin to strain.

Soon the flower is way up high,
Looking for the sun, big, round in the sky.
Then along comes the winter cold,
The flowers go down, where nothing grows.

Meghan Bone (9)
Ansdell Primary School, Lytham St Annes

Different Things I Like Best

Flowers are amazing, all red and round,
Flowers are amazing, scattered on the ground.

Tigers are fighting for their lunch,
Tigers are fighting in a bunch.

Teachers look good, like Captain Hook,
They all had a chance that they all took.

Jessica Beesley (9)
Ansdell Primary School, Lytham St Annes

Beauty

Beauty reminds me of flowers, like daisies and roses.
Beauty reminds me of nice pictures and people smiling at me.
Beauty reminds me of being kind and helpful.
Beauty reminds me of pretty petals shining in the sun.

Jackson Smith (7)
Ansdell Primary School, Lytham St Annes

Peace

Peace is blue, like the deep blue sea.
Peace smells like perfume floating through the air all around
the world.
Peace sounds like a fish wiggling towards the surface to you.
Peace feels like clean and soft washed hair.
Peace tastes like a glass of nice cold water.
Peace is beautiful and calm.

Alicia Holroyd (7)
Ansdell Primary School, Lytham St Annes

Video Games

Playing games all year round
Video games to be exact.
Lara Croft, guns and racing,
There is something to be found.
But I ask this question for the future,
Will you just answer this?
In the future will there be
Xbox 9000, PS360?
Only time will tell.
But in the year 2007,
I'm happy with my lot.
Xbox 360, PS3, Nintendo DS too.
There is one thing worrying me,
I'm already 52!

William Hutt (10)
Ansdell Primary School, Lytham St Annes

Under The Sea

Under the sea the fishes play,
Splash! Goes a dolphin,
On his way.
The crab goes *nip*!
The whale goes *bang!*
The sly, sly eel,
Tang-a-lang.
The coral is beautiful,
Green and red,
(There are mermaids there),
Or so they said.
The shells they use,
To comb their hair,
The sand flies up,
They couldn't care.
The seaweed sways,
To and fro,
There's chlorine there,
Down below.
So that is my under the sea,
So what? You might say,
(I wish it was me).

Bryony Whitaker (10)
Ansdell Primary School, Lytham St Annes

Animals

Animals are cuddly, cute and soft,
Dogs are playful,
Cats are colourful.

Some animals are scaly like a crocodile,
Rabbits are soft,
Hamsters are cute.

Some animals are smelly like an elephant,
Leopards are spotty,
Bears are hairy,
Animals are amazing!

Danielle Brooker (10)
Ansdell Primary School, Lytham St Annes

Captain Hook

Captain Hook had a look
At all the children's famous book costumes.
That's the one he wanted and then he pointed.
Who do you think the man is in fancy dress?
I think you should have a guess!
Who are the people dressed in colours?
I think you should have another guess too!

Matthew Smith-Ashman (10)
Ansdell Primary School, Lytham St Annes

Football

In football you need some space,
To get the ball, it is a race.
The ball is round and bouncy, it bounces everywhere,
If it bounces past you, it can catch you unaware.
Run down the wing to cross it in,
Or have a shot while they make a din.
The score is one-one, it's a draw,
I think this is the time to score.

Joe Frith-Jones (10)
Ansdell Primary School, Lytham St Annes

About The Earth

There are lots of people around the Earth,
Some days there are people giving birth.
Every day there are people dying,
While other people are crying.
There are lots of people under our feet,
And there are lots of places we can meet.
There are lots of people spitting,
As well as punching and hitting.
You don't always need money,
When you can make jam and honey.
On your computers there are lots of things to buy,
When you can go online.
There are lots of people who are starving,
Although they do lots of farming.
Lots of people say,
We need to work together every day.

Bradley Garner (10)
Ansdell Primary School, Lytham St Annes

The Forest

Forests,
I smell the
Waft of the oak
And pine tree's sap
Fresh from rainfall, smell
The flowers' berries that have just
Bloomed and ripened. Forests, hear
The faint flow of lapping streams or rivers,
Forests, hear the cheep of old and new birds,
Forests, feel the brush of wet leaves brush against your
Face, forests, feel your foot sink in the muddy marsh then
Squirt when you pull your feet out. Forests, feel the animals
Wriggle around near your feet in the leaves. Forests, touch
The fresh, slimy sap just out of the trees centre.
Touch the
Creatures
And insects
Of nature.
The forest.

Ross Philo (10)
Ansdell Primary School, Lytham St Annes

Everything In Sight

There's this girl in my class, I said,
Who eats like a chimpanzee
She eats:
Fruit cakes
Noodles
Oranges
Cookies
Apples
Scones
Chips
And more
Yesterday she even ate:
One pack of chalk
A notebook
A pencil
A table
A book
And even my teacher too.
So today our new teacher is here
She's really, really chubby
And today in maths
I heard a cry,
'Oh Mummy, you're here to stay!'

Helen Ruffley (10)
Ansdell Primary School, Lytham St Annes

Brothers And Sisters

Brothers, brothers, brothers
What are they like?
Brothers, brothers, brothers
They like to shout and fight!

Sisters, sisters, sisters
How great they would be
Sisters, sisters, sisters
I wish I could have three!

Emma Cowlishaw (10)
Ansdell Primary School, Lytham St Annes

The Roundabout Poem

Spinning fast
Round and round
Never want to stop
Looking up
Looking down
Makes me feel
Sick!
Like on a clock
And on a spaceship
Spinning fast
Round and round
It makes me feel happy
Spinning
Round and round
How I long to get off
But can't help myself to stay on
And spin
Round and round.

Hannah Smith (10)
Ansdell Primary School, Lytham St Annes

The Park

Can you hear the river flowing down the lane?
And the swans spread their snowy-white wings,
And does a dance to attract its friend.

Can you hear the crunch under your feet
As you step on the delicate, fallen leaves?
And the wind, blowing in the trees.

And just think of all the parks and land
That are being cut down right now
And all the trees that are used for paper.

Ruby Pemberton-Tingle (10)
Ansdell Primary School, Lytham St Annes

Nature

Water racing down a pebbled path.
The rich, golden corn blowing in calm, smooth breeze.
Hundreds of thousands of black and yellow bees
Making sugary, gorgeous honey for me.
The sight of a lovely old forest
By the mountains with snow at the top.
The big, wide ocean, not knowing what is out there.
The smell of green, green grass
Getting cut by the house, fierce flaming fires
Flickering in the fireplace while I go to bed.

Adam Mackle (10)
Ansdell Primary School, Lytham St Annes

How Do We Live Like This?

Trees decreasing without a choice
Animals eating anything they can see
Poison gas kills as it goes by.
Buildings ruin harmless animals' homes,
The sun melts the North Pole, global warming.

What is this world coming to?
We have to do something.

But trees, yes, are making furniture
And the animals need something to eat.
We can't do much about the air
And we need somewhere to live.
The sun makes us warmer, but
We have to do *something!*

Rebecca Evans (10)
Ansdell Primary School, Lytham St Annes

War

What is war?
What is war for?
People get killed by the ton
It is not fun
So stop!
So stop, this is war
We want it no more.

Ben Norris (10)
Ansdell Primary School, Lytham St Annes

The Playground

Look!
What can you see?
The swishing and swaying of giant evergreens,
The flying and gliding of old, dead leaves.

Listen!
What can you hear?
The cheeping and squawking of little garden birds.

Touch!
What can you feel?
The crisping and crackling of dry, brown leaves,
The spikes and sprigs of prickly holly.

William Anderton (9)
Braithwaite CE (VA) Primary School, Keswick

The Playground

Look!
What do you see?
The mountains
With bracken and moss
Full of happiness and glee,.

Listen!
What do you hear?
The birds cheeping
In the mulberry bush
Happy as can be.

Touch!
What do you feel?
Leaves all crinkly
Falling off the trees.

Savour!
What do you taste?
The wind blowing on my tongue
And my cold face.

Sniff!
What do you smell?
The air blowing up my nose
And freezing my cold skin.

Emily Cartmell (9)
Braithwaite CE (VA) Primary School, Keswick

Playtime

Look!
What can you see?
Nettles
Moving in the wind
Swishing side to side.

Listen!
What can you hear?
Birds
Singing quietly
A lovely song.

Joe Clark (9)
Braithwaite CE (VA) Primary School, Keswick

Playground

Look!
What do you see?
The red-hot sun
Burning your eyes
And melting
The school down.

Listen!
What do you hear?
The A66
With cars accelerating.

Sniff!
What do you smell?
The clouds' breeze
Going up my nose.

Touch!
What do you feel?
A frozen sand box
With slippery, wet ice.

Connor Clarke (8)
Braithwaite CE (VA) Primary School, Keswick

Trees In The Playground

Trees are green
Trees are brown
You never know if
They're going to smile or frown.

And when their leaves
Swoop off the trees
You never know where
They're going to be!

Rhiannon Davies (9)
Braithwaite CE (VA) Primary School, Keswick

Playground

Look!
What can you see?
The red-hot sun
Burning your eyes
And melting your school bag.

Listen!
What can you hear?
The sound of children shouting
And a faraway bird shouting at me.

Touch!
What can you feel?
The boiling hot sun on my face
And the hedge rustling.

Sniff!
What can you smell?
The nice breeze
On a good summer's day.

Tommy Edmondson (9)
Braithwaite CE (VA) Primary School, Keswick

The Playtime Poem

Look!
What do you see?
Tiny little grass blades
On the field so green.

Listen!
What can you hear?
Birds singing
In my ear.

Savour!
What do you taste?
The very cold air
As thin as a piece of hair.

Look!
What do you see?
Sparkling ice
Just like me.

Listen!
What do you hear?
Chattering of people
Not so very near.

Savour!
What do you taste?
Fresh wind
Blowing in my face.

Zoë Lord (8)
Braithwaite CE (VA) Primary School, Keswick

Wintertime

Look!
What can you see?
Rain swishing
On swaying evergreens.

Touch!
What can you feel?
Fresh wind
Blowing into my face.

Listen!
What can you hear?
Frost crunching
As people walk by.

Touch!
What can you feel?
Crunchy leaves
Blowing into my feet.

Look!
What can you see?
Leaves forever
Falling off trees.

Matthew McMorrow (9)
Braithwaite CE (VA) Primary School, Keswick

Look!

Look!
What do you see?
A tree swishing in the snow
Or the night weather in the starry sky.

Look!
What do you see?
Splashing through the puddles
Through the wet weather.

Look!
What do you see?
I can see a tree swishing in the sky
I can hear the twittering birds in the sky
Flying and swooping around.

Listen!
What do you hear?
I can hear the squirrels
Chewing the nuts open
I can hear the dogs barking
And swishing through the days.

Charlie Mattinson (8)
Braithwaite CE (VA) Primary School, Keswick

Nature

Swaying trees
Busy bees
Smooth or rough plants

Spiky moss
Tweety birds
All big and small

Tasty air
Bright flowers
Dull or really bright

Rough or smooth
Big and small
Dull or really bright
Doesn't matter what they are
They're just all *nature!*

Jessica Pepper (8)
Braithwaite CE (VA) Primary School, Keswick

The Playground

Listen!
What do you hear?
Little robin redbreasts
Twittering in my ear.

Stop!
What do you feel?
Tiny weaving plants
On a rough wooden wheel.

Taste!
What do you sense?
The cold winter wind
Like freezing little crystals.

Look!
What do you see?
Lots and lots of chimneys
Puffing and huffing with smoke.

Hannah Yare (9)
Braithwaite CE (VA) Primary School, Keswick

Look!

Listen!
What do you hear?
Children screaming and shouting.

Look!
What do you see?
Children playing football.

Touch!
What can you feel?
Smooth cherries,
Prickly holly.

Touch!
What can you feel?
Spiky grass.

Look!
What do you see?
Green grass,
Brown, muddy mud.

Hugh Blakemore (7)
Braithwaite CE (VA) Primary School, Keswick

Come Outside

Look!
What do you see?
The trees blowing wild
And it's blowing my hair
High up into the sky.

Look!
What do you see?
A fish swimming in a pool
And it's bigger than me.

Listen!
What do you hear?
The heaters humming
And they're louder than me.

Touch!
What can you feel?
The rock-hard table
And it's rock, rock hard.

Georgina Clark (7)
Braithwaite CE (VA) Primary School, Keswick

Use Your Senses

Look!
What do you see?
The clouds are puffy
They blow in the cloudy air.

Listen!
What do you hear?
The birds singing
In the old, still standing trees.

Natalie Field (8)
Braithwaite CE (VA) Primary School, Keswick

The Playground

Listen!
What do you hear?
Crinkly leaves
Crunching in your hand
The whistling wind
Blowing around.

Stop!
What can you feel?
Bumpy leaves
Whirling and twirling
Holly leaves
Spiky and smooth.

Look!
What do you see?
The fluffy, puffy clouds
Floating by
And the chimney
Puffing out smoke.

Bethan Hughes (7)
Braithwaite CE (VA) Primary School, Keswick

Look!

Look!
What can you see?
A big round caterpillar
Chewing on a leaf
As shiny as a block of gold.

Listen!
What can you hear?
Crackly, crunchy leaves
As pale as pale can be.
Slishy, sloshy mud
Reduced to sludge.

Jon-Paul Marley (8)
Braithwaite CE (VA) Primary School, Keswick

Playground Poem

Look!
What can you see?
I can see wind blowing in the trees
And the washing
Swinging backwards and forwards.

Listen!
What can you hear?
A bird singing beautifully in the tree,
An aeroplane zooming in the sky.

Look!
What can you see?
Twinkling windows of a house
And brown flowers dying on the ground.

Amy Oxley (8)
Braithwaite CE (VA) Primary School, Keswick

Come On!

Listen!
What do you hear?
The wind whistling in the treetops.

Look!
What do you see?
Kids playing hopping and skipping.

Touch!
What do you feel?
The trees with all their bumps and lumps.

Timmy Price (8)
Braithwaite CE (VA) Primary School, Keswick

The Playground

Look!
What do you see?
The wind swishing in your face.

Listen!
What do you hear?
The quiet tweeting of a calm bird.

Savour!
What do you taste?
The fresh wind blowing raindrops onto my tongue.

Sniff!
What do you smell?
I can smell grass, all fresh and cold.

Touch!
What do you feel?
The leaves all slimy in my hand.

Robert Saxton (7)
Braithwaite CE (VA) Primary School, Keswick

Come On Outside

Listen!
What do you hear?
The birds singing and whispering in my ear.

Look!
What do you see?
Birds sitting on the new, growing trees.

Touch!
What do you feel?
Wet, slimy grass in a beautiful field.

Britani Stuart (8)
Braithwaite CE (VA) Primary School, Keswick

Monday's Child

Monday's child plays in the shed
Tuesday's child stays in bed
Wednesday's child plays in the rain
Thursday's child goes on a train
Friday's child wets the bed
Saturday's child bangs his head
But the child that is born on the Sabbath day
Is kind and nice and loves to play.

Eleanor Bird (8)
Brotherton & Byram CP School, Brotherton

The Day The Zoo Escaped

The tiger rushed out happily
The panda crept out lazily

The kangaroo hopped out quickly
The elephant stomped out loudly

The snake slid out scarily
The cheetah pounced out weirdly

But the giraffe stubbornly
Just stayed where it was.

Ellie Atkinson (9)
Brotherton & Byram CP School, Brotherton

Song Of The Jumbo Jet

You see the jumbo jet on the runway
Revving its engine like a growling lion
It looks like a bird catching its prey
People packed in like biscuits and can't move
Floating in the air like a feather.

Jake Edwards (8)
Brotherton & Byram CP School, Brotherton

Christmas

C hristmas time is here again
H olly berries on the tree
R udolph's on his way
I vy wreaths on the door
S now is falling on the floor
T oys and presents waiting to be opened
M um's cooking dinner
A new baby is born
S anta's here.

Nathan Williamson (9)
Brotherton & Byram CP School, Brotherton

The Magnificent . . .

The magnificent rhino
My rhino is grey like a thunder cloud
His roar is like a strike of lightning
His head is like a ball of stone
His legs are like pillars of steel
He resembles a metal tank
I will protect you
So wherever you go you are not afraid.

Ciara Wilson (9)
Brotherton & Byram CP School, Brotherton

Song Of The Gallardo

You see the Gallardo in the garage
The engine is doing its best like school work
The yellow car racing round the track like a cheetah
The wheels spin like a boomerang
The steering wheel leaning in and out
Like a monkey swinging.

Tyger Watkins (8)
Brotherton & Byram CP School, Brotherton

Song Of The Motorbike

You see the motorbike on the track
Roar like a lion in the jungle
The wheel spins like a blade
The handlebars twist and turn like a tornado
The exhaust bounces like people jumping.

Daniel Rawden (8)
Brotherton & Byram CP School, Brotherton

All In Red

Red for Santa's fur-lined coat
And his scarlet hood
Red for the holly berries
Gleaming in the wood
Red for the breast
Of the bravest little bird
Red for the brightest Christmas word

Red for the tip of Rudolph's nose
And for the decorations on the tree
That Mum put on today
Red for lights
On Santa's sleigh
Red for the sparkling Christmas wine
Placed on the top table for when we dine

Red for the glow of the yule log light
And the little crimson slippers
That Santa left last night
Red for the paper lanterns
Hanging from the wall
Of the many Christmas colours
Red's the best of all.

Amy Stockhill (9)
Brotherton & Byram CP School, Brotherton

The Magnificent . . .

The magnificent elephant
My elephant is fat and round like a grey cloud in the sky
His big ears are like a coloured leaf on a tree
His tusk is like a big thorn on the bush
His clumpy feet are like big hard rocks at the seaside
He resembles a giant grey monster
I will feed him with giant lumps of food every day.

Amy Lawton (9)
Brotherton & Byram CP School, Brotherton

Monday's Child

Monday's child lies in bed
Tuesday's child likes wearing red
Wednesday's child loves eating stew
Thursday's child loves Scooby-Doo
Friday's child is kind and caring
Saturday's child likes sharing
But the child that's born on the Sabbath day
Is good and helpful, but will turn grey.

Amy Bastow (9)
Brotherton & Byram CP School, Brotherton

The Magnificent . . .

The magnificent lion
My lion is orange like the evening sunset
His fur is like the hair on my chest
His claws are like knives
His eyes are like mud in the garden
He resembles the savannah grass and the Sahara desert
I will guard him with my rifle.

Matthew Barker (9)
Brotherton & Byram CP School, Brotherton

Gently

Gently I float in the nice blue sea
Gently I listen to lovely soft music
Gently I stroke my pet on the back
Gently I get into bed and go to sleep

Gently I tie my hair up in a bun
Gently I feel the soft grass
Gently is the cat's tail
But the gentlest of all . . .
My cat cuddling me.

Alice Lawton (9)
Brotherton & Byram CP School, Brotherton

Quickly

Quickly the cat runs on land
Quickly the antelope crosses the sand
Quickly the nerve endings go to my feet
Quickly the pen crosses my sheet

Quickly the greyhound runs in the race
Quickly a smile comes across my face
Quick as a shooting star
But the quickest of all . . .
Is David Beckham crossing a ball.

Sasha Flanagan (9)
Brotherton & Byram CP School, Brotherton

Guess Who?

Belly poker
Head breaker
Shell cracker
Spoon disliker
Bread hater
Yolk spiller
Wall jumper
Long dropper
Bottom smasher
Glue lover.

Answer: Humpty Dumpty.

Joshua Thomas (9)
Brotherton & Byram CP School, Brotherton

Waterfall

Rumbling, tumbling, grumbling
The water cascaded down.
Twisting, swirling, whirling
The water spins around.
The waterfall flows like a dolphin
Darting in the sea.
Jumping, playing, chasing
As happy as can be.

Annabel Noble (9)
Brotherton & Byram CP School, Brotherton

Cat

Rat chaser
Tail shaker
Paw pouncer
Good bouncer
Tree climber
Mouse timer
Nose twitcher
Food snitcher
Day sleeper
Night seeker.

Katie Pidgeon (10)
Brotherton & Byram CP School, Brotherton

The School Sound Collector

(Based on 'The Sound Collector' by Roger McGough)

'A stranger called this morning
Dressed all in black and grey
Put every sound into a bag
And carried it away.'

The ticking of the clock
The bouncing of the ball
The squeaking of the chairs
The singing in the hall

The playing of the music
The rattling of the gate
The ringing of the bell
The shouting of mate

'A stranger called this morning
He didn't leave his name
Left us only silence
Life will never be the same.'

William Glover (9)
Brotherton & Byram CP School, Brotherton

My Dream

Yesterday a bird sang to me,
I noticed he had a flea,
He jumped up and down,
While wearing a crown.

He flew away so I followed on my bike,
But then up popped a pike,
He punched me in the face
And that was when I lost all trace.

The next thing I knew,
My mum was shouting, 'School!'
But the strange thing was,
The dog was playing pool.

Jake Barker (10)
Brotherton & Byram CP School, Brotherton

Spiders

Spiders are small,
Spiders are black,
They have hairs on their back,
A spider can attack.
They can climb up a backpack,
They can't eat a flapjack,
Or else they would have a whack
On their back,
Or they would die from a delicious snack.

Jack Croft (10)
Brotherton & Byram CP School, Brotherton

Football Poem

If you think you can shoot
Try winning the golden boot
Get off your bum
And stop playing the flute.

If you think you can score
Make sure that you're sure
That you can score
Past Bobby Moore.

Nick Banks (11)
Brotherton & Byram CP School, Brotherton

A Day At The Waterpark

Slip 'n' slide
Snorkel or
Dive, there's
Loads of fun
Things to do!
Splish 'n' splosh
Go down
A slide
Or sit on
The side,
While you
Watch all the children laugh
And play!
If you're having fun, go sunbathe in
The sun and relax until it's time to
Go back home.
Y
A
H
O
O!

Harrison France (10)
Brotherton & Byram CP School, Brotherton

Kitten

K itten, kitten
I n a ball, sleeping
T wisting and twirling
T hieves my meat
E normous tail
N aughty and mischievous.

Lynda Lindley (9)
Brotherton & Byram CP School, Brotherton

Horse Poem - Kennings

Grass eater
Apple feaster
Fast trotter
Slow plodder

Carrot cruncher
Sugarbeet muncher
Low jumper
High jumper

Swaying walker
Bouncing trotter
Speeding canterer
Lively galloper.

Tanya Carroll (9)
Brotherton & Byram CP School, Brotherton

The Magnificent . . .

The magnificent rhino
My rhino is black, like sea on the beach
His charge is like the speed of a car
His horns are like a big ice cream cone
His ears are like little pastel sweets
He resembles a teddy bear
I will keep him safe when he is in danger.

Rebecca Littler (9)
Brotherton & Byram CP School, Brotherton

My Grandma Saw A Rugby-Playing Hippo

My grandma saw a rugby-playing hippo
At the park on a day in March
The captain said we'll have him 'ditto'
And the cheerleaders shouted as they came from the arch.

My grandma said he didn't have to run
He walked all the way and shook the ground as he swayed
They all had a lot of fun and so did the nun
They all had a break and so they lay.

They said he was good
You would win us the match
Even though you eat mud
You would lead us in our march.

My grandma said that she sat down
And then they followed me
All the way round the town
Now I'm glad I get the game I see,
So come on, hippo,
Stop following me!

Lucy Golding (11)
Brotherton & Byram CP School, Brotherton

Best Friend

B rilliant
E xciting
S uperb
T errific and trustful

F riends forever
R eally groovy
I maginative
E xtremely entertaining
N ever-ending friendship
D ear friend.

Lauren Reid (9)
Brotherton & Byram CP School, Brotherton

Feelings

Fear is black like the smell of burning and the sound of grinding,
Love is pink like the heart of love and the sound of kissing,
Silence is white with nothing to feel and nothing to smell,
Sadness is dark blue when you are all alone,
Happiness is yellow, is a spot of yellow,
Anger is purple like the growl of a dog,
Fun is light blue with everyone cheery.

Charlotte Anderson (10)
Etherley Lane CP School, Bishop Auckland

Lost

Kisses fill the air,
Laughter lifts me up,
The sound of fun,
Talking to my friends.

But all of a sudden I'm lost,
No one near, no one there.

Silence fills the air,
A quiet song far away,
Only the tune to be heard.

The sadness of me is making me fear,
A teardrop falls from my eyes.

Back from my journey I am,
The laughter, the fun I enjoy.
How happy to be home!

Heather Bruhlmann (10)
Etherley Lane CP School, Bishop Auckland

A River Of Feelings

Darkness, dark and black and the taste of poison.
Fear, burning black like the sound of a barking dog.
Love, like a river of melted chocolate and filled with happiness.
Hate, with the red blaze of a roaring fire.
Happiness, the sound of laughing, the smell of clean, fresh air
and the colour of yellow.
Sadness, like a candle with the light about to go out, and the
moaning of a lonely voice.

Daniel Quigley (10)
Etherley Lane CP School, Bishop Auckland

Sadness

The sadness of brown dread and sorrow
With sympathy leaking out of my heart.
Oh, but the anger of burgundy spikes and squeals,
Black hate and the taste of smoke!
The fear building in me of the red happiness of love,
With the taste of summer fruits,
The silence, oh nothing was said in that white room,
Then what was that moment when happiness came,
When yellow laughing and the taste of cakes and sweets
Seeped into my mouth?
Then darkness overcame me once again,
Bright red darkness,
Almost like life was taken away.

Bethany Jane Salt (10)
Etherley Lane CP School, Bishop Auckland

A Happy Ending

Love was in the air,
I felt the pinkness of hugs and red roses slowly growing.
Yet sadness was in the dark clouds
And tears were coming from a delicate daisy.
The laughing of friends,
As white as a fragile white rose growing,
As delicate as a snowflake.

Anger came slowly, slithering like a sly snake,
Whilst a pansy died in the darkness.
Then happiness came and made the world bright,
While sunflowers smiled brightly,
Bringing smiles back everywhere,
Making flowers smile all around the world.

Millie Allison (11)
Etherley Lane CP School, Bishop Auckland

Feelings

Hate is black, shouting and burning.
Fear is blue, grinding and burning.
Anger is dark red, like red blood.
Love is red, like chocolate.

Daniel Cooper (11)
Etherley Lane CP School, Bishop Auckland

The Way Of The World

Feelings are all around,
They are in who we are and what we do.
They can be a dark blue sea of fear, heart beating fast,
A white feeling of love for everyone to own,
An orange hate that is strong and as deep as a blow to the heart,
Or a happiness, yellow as the sun
beaming on a beach of golden sand,
A sadness, grey, a girl weeping, bewildered with life,
An anger, red, burning fire, head pounding, Earth shaking

A silence, lilac, only the sound of your life rushing behind you,
Or a fun, green, Christmas morning, a good feeling deep inside,
A hunger, needing something to stop the emptiness, brown,
A sound of laughter, a cheerful child, pink,
Or a darkness, black, river gushing, coming closer and closer,
What feelings are your lives made out of?

Maria Street (11)
Etherley Lane CP School, Bishop Auckland

Feelings

Black as fear, the sound of grinding and the smell of burning,
Yellow as happiness, the sound of merriment, the smell of joy,
Red as anger, the sound of rage, the touch of fear,
Orange as laughter, the sound of laughing, the touch of humour,
Blue as fun, the sound of enjoyment, the touch of joy.

David Batty (11)
Etherley Lane CP School, Bishop Auckland

Darkness Or Light

The purple sky full of fear, volcano burning, fires raging
The sky, setting, smells of roses in the air,
Putting a rose in your wife's hair,
The world gone red, scowling fills the air,
Hearing the screams of hate from the dreaded enemy,
The world gone silent, not a peep,
As shepherds round up their sheep,
Feelings of darkness that come with the night,
Or feelings of happiness that come with the light,
All of these feelings, dark or light
Make us human and give us our rights.

Ben Wigham (11)
Etherley Lane CP School, Bishop Auckland

Burst Out

I can feel the fear when I hear
The sound of the swords clanging, the smell of burning,
Sadness takes me over
With the sound of nothing,
Darkness is here.
With the screaming and the fear,
Hate tastes bitter inside.
Like it's pulling you down, down to the ground,
Happiness makes you spring into the air.
Like you don't care,
Love is different.
It makes you feel all warm inside,
Fun, fun, you can never get away
From fun!
Laughter makes you sing, sing into silence.

Stacey Johnson (10)
Etherley Lane CP School, Bishop Auckland

Feelings

I can feel the fear when I hear
The sounds of grinding metal, the smell of burning.
Love is different, it makes you feel lovely inside.
Fun, fun, joyful fun, you can have fun all night long.
Laughter is like jumping up and down,
Like you are a Jack-in-the-box.
Hunger is like bacon as my tummy rumbles.
Happiness is like the wind blowing through your hair.

Kane Grant (10)
Etherley Lane CP School, Bishop Auckland

How Do You Feel?

Fear is grey, I hear screams and burning,
Love is red, I hear kisses from mother to child, I smell roses,
Hate is swamp-green, I hear boiling pots, I smell sour city fumes,
Happiness is yellow, it laughs at me, I can smell the sweet scent
of perfume,
Sadness is light blue, I hear sobs from a crying baby, I smell salt,
Anger is brown, I hear growls and I smell a bitter sour smell,
Silence is white, I hear a drip from a tap, I smell disinfectant,
Hunger is peach, I hear friends munching, I don't want to eat,
The smell of chocolate is overpowering, I need to eat.

But one question - how do *you* feel?

Lydia Samuel (10)
Etherley Lane CP School, Bishop Auckland

Colours Of My Mind

Darkness is black with the smell of nothing,
Anger is red, groaning with the smell of flames,
Happiness is yellow, the sound of laughter and the smell of flowers,
Fun is orange, cheerful and the smell of freshly baked cakes,
Love is pink with the scent of roses and the sound of kisses
From mothers to children.

Chloe Wearmouth (10)
Etherley Lane CP School, Bishop Auckland

A Mixture Of Feelings

Love is sweet like chocolate and cuddly like a panda,
Hate is a hurtful green or the shout of a hateful shark,
Sadness is blue like the sky or a rainbow fish's cry,
Anger is like a tiger, it roars but it feels no hate,
When you laugh with a smile on your face,
You know you're in the right place.
Be as silent as a deer, but have no fear,
Glow bright when you have fun in the sun with your friends.
The world is a mixture of feelings.

Amy Hart (10)
Etherley Lane CP School, Bishop Auckland

Senses

Fear is the red scream of a burning spider.
Love is the sound of a pink, singing bird.
Hate is the screech of a horrid black bat.
Happiness is the sound of music from a yellow cat.
Darkness is nothing, but just a sour, black snake.
And fun is the sound of kids laughing and talking
To their cute and cuddly pets.

Callam Newcombe (11)
Etherley Lane CP School, Bishop Auckland

When Fear Turns Into Fun!

Fear is burning inside of me like a hot, roasting fire
Hate is all around me, it goes bang and boom in the night,
Sadness, I cry, making puddles like pools of water,
Hunger, I have, you can hear the rumbling in my tummy a mile away,
I'm in the darkness all day long, shivers run up my spine,
Silence is around, don't ever speak one single word.

Happiness I have, I'm free, I'm free, I'm free,
I can feel love once more when I smell one delicate rose.
Fun, fun, fun is what I have now,
I can laugh all I like - *I'm free!*

Danielle Gillett (11)
Etherley Lane CP School, Bishop Auckland

Key Stage 2

Scared, scared,
Lovely toast,
I hate peanuts,
Try not to boast.

Nervous, nervous,
Get to school gate,
Go faster, Dad,
I'm very late.

Excited, excited,
It's playtime now,
Let's play tig,
Reception say how?

Bored, bored,
It's art,
Let's make it fun,
Draw Bart.

Lunch, lunch,
Wait in line,
Don't punch,
It's not a crime.

Afternoon, afternoon,
We have some work,
Writing down a million times,
'You're a jerk'.

Home time, home time,
I'm so happy,
Waiting for my mum to pick me up,
Oh no, we have to change my brother's nappy.

Joshua Edozien (8)
Greenfield St Mary's Primary School, Oldham

My First Day

Excited, excited, mustn't be late,
Leave the house at half-past eight.

Excited, excited, when I get older,
I will be much, much colder.

Dinner, dinner, mustn't be late,
Gobble food before it's too late.

Home time, home time, we all say hooray,
And do star of the day.

Luke Castle (7)
Greenfield St Mary's Primary School, Oldham

My First Day

Excited, excited, mustn't be late
Got to go at half-past eight.
Excited, excited, got to be on time,
Teacher might be in a line.

Excited, excited, assembly is starting,
Got to be first to sing departing.
Excited, excited, I've got a new teacher,
I'm really excited and ready to meet her.

Excited, excited, the whistle has blown,
I'm really, really hungry and ready to eat.
Dinner's over, ready to learn.

I need new books, I'll wait my turn,
Excited, excited, school is over,
Got to go in my Rover.

Jake Howarth (7)
Greenfield St Mary's Primary School, Oldham

Back To School

Excited, excited, nervous I am,
Excited, excited, quickly
Quickly get up,
Get into my new uniform,
Quickly, come on,
Down to the kitchen making my breakfast,
Oh no, it's all gone.

Excited, excited, nervous I am,
Excited, excited, quickly, come on,
Into the porch, getting my shoes,
Putting them on,
As they shone,
Unhook my coat,
Put it on.

Excited, excited, nervous I am,
Excited, excited, quickly, come on,
Go outside,
Into the cold,
Soon I arrive at the school gate,
By half-past eight,
Oh, I'm late!

Excited, excited, nervous I am,
Excited, excited, quickly, come on,
Get into class,
I walk into class,
'Why are you late?'
'Sorry,' I explained,
'I arrived at the gate
By half-past eight.'

I have my playtime,
We can go out,
We can play on the roundabout.
It soon turns 12,
It is now dinner time,
Run outside and get first to go
On the roundabout.

It is art, it is art,
We have to draw a cart.
We had fun all day,
Now it is time for star of the day.
'Wow! Well done, Fay.'

Get our bags and coats,
Line up,
Quick,
Go outside, see our mum,
I said,
'I had fun, Mum.'

Lucy Brewster (7)
Greenfield St Mary's Primary School, Oldham

I Am Really Nervous

Nervous, nervous,
It's a different day,
Get to school,
Out outside and play.

Nervous, nervous,
The bell rings,
First in assembly,
We are to sing.

Nervous, nervous,
Go down the stairs,
Now we are going to do our doubles,
So stand on your chairs.

Nervous, nervous,
It is playtime,
Why don't we rhyme?

Nervous, nervous,
We've had lots of fun,
It's so shiny
Because of the sun.

Nervous, nervous,
It's nearly dinner,
Maybe it will
Make me simmer.

Nervous, nervous,
Now it's art,
We are going to draw
An enormous cart.

Nervous, nervous,
Who's star of the day?
Tim,
Because he has been working well with him.

Nervous, nervous,
Oh, Mum,
The food was really yum.

Nervous, nervous,
My dad is mad,
But I am glad
About the day I had.

Anna Edmondson (7)
Greenfield St Mary's Primary School, Oldham

My First Day At School

When I go to school, it's just like playing pool.
In the playground, just like a lion strides across the ground.

Excited, excited, I am ready for dinner,
The food has got healthier,
I'm going outside,
All that exercise will make me slimmer.

We're going back into school, here we come,
Excited, excited, listen to the teacher, I'm trying to be cool.

Home time, home time,
Got to get a move on, football training is tonight.

Clayton Thomas (8)
Greenfield St Mary's Primary School, Oldham

My First Day Ever

Nervous, nervous, no need to be
Oh my gosh, I am in class 3,
Hurry, hurry, I am a little late,
I need to run faster
So I can get to the gate.

I am looking forward
To seeing my friends,
Playing with them,
Never ends.

The teacher says every day,
She likes this class in a way,
I don't know if it's the way,
They sit and fiddle with their sticks.

Playing, playing in the school,
I can't believe it,
It's so very cool.
This game is great,
I can't wait,
To have a new mate.

Lunch, lunch is now,
Go in the line,
You are wasting time,
Up they walk,
Very proud.

Afternoon, afternoon,
We are doing a song,
Musical instruments,
She goes *bong!*

Home time, home time is sad,
It has come so quick,
But people feel glad.

Nikita Johnson (7)
Greenfield St Mary's Primary School, Oldham

Excited, Excited

Excited, excited
Mustn't be late
Gobble crunchy cornflakes
Out of the gate
Arrive at half-past eight
I bet it'll be great.

Excited, excited
Now I'm at school
I wonder if
I'll be able to play pool.

Excited, excited
It's playtime!
Let's run outside
And wait for my clock to chime.

Excited, excited
Back to work
I hope our teacher
Will make us jerk.

Excited, excited
Let's run out
Let's go and shout
On the roundabout.

Excited, excited
Run inside
Let's look out of the window
For a slide.

Excited, excited
Who's going to be
Star of the day?
Maybe it'll be Fay.

Excited, excited
I shouted to Mum
Have you brought me
Any gum?

James Mallinson (7)
Greenfield St Mary's Primary School, Oldham

Excited For School

Excited, excited
Mustn't be late
School starts
At half-past eight.

Excited, excited
Mustn't be late
The food's gonna be healthy
So you're not going to faint.

Excited, excited
We're back at school
I really think
I could rule.

Excited, excited
I'm listening now
The teacher is teaching
Really, but how?

Excited, excited
Ready for dinner
The food's healthy
To make me slimmer.

Excited, excited
Ready for home
When I get there
I will play with the toy phone.

Ben Gardner (7)
Greenfield St Mary's Primary School, Oldham

My First Day

Bell time, bell time
I am late
He is annoying
The brother I hate.

Scared, scared
The gate is closed
Teacher won't be happy
Because she's a mean chappie.

Happy, happy
My name's Sappy
Meeting friends old and new
But who is he? Who, who, who?

Surprised, surprised
Dinner time already
Walk for dinner
But very steady.

Home time, home time
Everyone's gone
But Mum is very late
She gets me at half-past one!

Samuel Doyle (7)
Greenfield St Mary's Primary School, Oldham

My Cool School

Excited, excited, got no time
Got to leave at half-past nine.

Excited, excited, I know I am late,
'Mum, what time will I be at the gate?'

Excited, excited, I am at the gate
The teacher asks me why I'm late.

Excited, excited, I get my new books
Excited, excited, I think I've got new looks.

Excited, excited, I'm ready for dinner
Excited, excited, I think I've got slimmer.

Excited, excited, ready for art
Excited, excited, what shall I paint next, a man's heart.

Excited, excited, time to go home
Excited, excited, I realise I'm not alone.

James Burrington-Collins (7)
Greenfield St Mary's Primary School, Oldham

I'm Ready For School

Quick, quick,
Mustn't be late,
Eat my toast
Before half-past eight.

Leave the house,
Before I'm late,
I need to be
At the gate.

Quick, quick,
At the school but I'm late,
The teacher
Won't be feeling great.

Playtime is great,
When you shout and play,
But it's best
When you're feeling great.

Work, work, it's not so great,
When you have sums like
Eight times eight
And nine times nine.

Dinner time, dinner time,
It's so great,
When you play out
With all your mates.

Home time, home time,
It's the best,
When you go home
And play with your friends.

Reuben Whyatt (7)
Greenfield St Mary's Primary School, Oldham

My First Day

When I started Year 3
I was seven,
But when I go to secondary school,
I will be eleven.

Learning starts at an early age
And my knowledge grows,
As I reach each stage.

When I moved from infants to juniors,
I was filled with anxiety,
But shorter playtimes
And longer working times
Was the reality.

After working in the morning,
It's time for my dinner,
Healthy food, fresh air and exercise,
Will help me stay thinner.

Literacy, numeracy, topic and art,
We have to make a big chart.
Before I enter college,
I will cram my mind with knowledge.

James Howard (8)
Greenfield St Mary's Primary School, Oldham

If I . . .

If I had eyes then I could see,
The flowers growing prettily.

If I had ears then I could hear,
Children laughing loud and clear.

If I had a nose then I could smell,
My mother's cooking I know so well.

If I had a mouth then I could taste,
Chocolate bars with all good haste.

If I had hands then I could touch,
My puppy dog I love so much.

But wait a minute, oh yippee!
I have all these senses in my body.
So I can shout with so much glee,
If I could be anyone, then I would be . . . *me!*

Bethany Roberts (9)
Greenfield St Mary's Primary School, Oldham

My First Day In Year 3

My first day in Year 3
Was just like throwing a ball at the tree
Listen to the teacher, trying to be cool
I wonder if I'll get time to play pool?

Playtime is here
What a cheer
Making new friends
Never ends.

Back to work
With a jerk
In art
I drew a heart.

Lunch, lunch
What a time to give someone a punch
On the roundabout, round and round
The girl shouts out loud.

In the afternoon
The sky shines like the moon
Home time's here
But Mum is nowhere.

Aysha Brannon (7)
Greenfield St Mary's Primary School, Oldham

I'm Ready For School

I'm ready, I'm ready
No time to lose
I have to be in my line
For half-past nine.

I'm ready, I'm ready
I am in my classroom
I have a new teacher
And I am ready to meet her.

I'm ready, I'm ready
The bell rings for food
In my packed lunch the food is healthy
So it makes me slim.

I'm ready, I'm ready
I am in my classroom
I need new books so I wait my turn
And I am ready to learn.

I'm ready, I'm ready
It's home time
Who is star of the day?

Emma Sykes (7)
Greenfield St Mary's Primary School, Oldham

My Last Journey

Still time to turn around
    Don't want to go
    Can't make me go
    Don't need to go
Marched down the lane
To imminent doom
Another step closer
To my terrible fate
    Don't want to go
    Can't make me go
    Don't need to go
I hear a klaxon
Calling inmates to
Roll call
Inside the concrete building
    Don't want to go
    Can't make me go
    Don't need to go
To school.

May Wall (11)
Greenfield St Mary's Primary School, Oldham

The Terrible Trip

The terrible trip to ski,
With Bro, Grandma, Grandad and me,
Grandma fell and broke her back,
The supervisor got the sack.

Grandad tried some hot, hot sauce,
Rushed to the bathroom with such a force,
My bro and me were left alone,
Our tummies began to grunt and groan,

Left with no money to spend,
This terrible trip was not going to end,
Terrible trip!

Emma Ferguson (10)
Greenfield St Mary's Primary School, Oldham

School

It's time to go to school
Sigh, what a drool

The teachers are so mean
They won't let you breathe

The dinners are horrid slime
They are a crime

Hooray, it's home time again
I can have a lie in until half ten.

Kristian Longden (11)
Greenfield St Mary's Primary School, Oldham

When The Aliens Stole My Undies

When the aliens stole my undies
They stole them off my line,
They were drying off quite nicely
But now they're flying high.

I wish they would come back
My blue, stripy ones,
They were my favourites
But now they're probably green.

What can I do
If I really need the loo?
What would I do
Without my blues?

I'll have to use my reds instead
But I wet them when I was in bed.
My blues were nice and clean
But now they're a slimy green.

The aliens did it overnight
When I was sleeping, wrapped up tight.

Fay Taylor (10)
Greenfield St Mary's Primary School, Oldham

Looking Glass

Trudging through a bed of crisp
A frozen ice land, a candy wisp
Even in the northern hemisphere
Once a year the lights appear
The sky is misty, it is hard to see
What the world means to me
Staring through the looking glass
I remember everything in my past!

Rowanne Walker-Heap (11)
Greenfield St Mary's Primary School, Oldham

Bedtime Snack

Tiptoe out of bed at night
Creep out of the eerie sight
Go downstairs in the kitchen now
Walking onward you slowly plough
Through the open door the fridge awaits
Going past some dirty plates
You open silently the fridge door
You reach for something you adore
Chocolate . . .

Hannah Claydon (10)
Greenfield St Mary's Primary School, Oldham

Guess Who?

Champion racer
Oat chaser
Jump shaker
Oat taker
Riding cracker
Oat snacker
Perfect rider
Oat hider
Night snoozer
Oat loser
Morning reminder
Next rider!
What am I?

Answer: one white horse.

Meera Khiroya (10)
Greenfield St Mary's Primary School, Oldham

Sea Horses

You see them in pools
You see them upon the shore
They bob up and down
So we can see
What lies beneath the dark blue sea
Swim down deep
Then we can seek
Those horses deep.

Alice Frost (10)
Greenfield St Mary's Primary School, Oldham

My Feelings

When I am feeling happy
When I am feeling sad
When someone hurts my feelings
I get really, really mad.

Feelings make me laugh
Feelings make me cry
Feelings make me ordinary
Sometimes I wonder why.

Sometimes you keep feelings to yourself
Feelings are always there
But when you're with your best friends
Feelings are there to share.

Teegan Cowley Merrington (10)
Greenfield St Mary's Primary School, Oldham

My Dog, Blossom

My name is Blossom, I love to play,
I go for a walk every day.
Sometimes up and sometimes down,
I also love to run around.
I fetch the stick thrown for me,
By my owner called Molly.
My favourite game is tug-of-war,
I hold on tight and give a roar.
I always like to win this game,
But Molly wins and then we start again.
I am good at tricks, like shake a paw,
And roll over like a ball.
On shopping day it's good fun,
Molly buys me a chocolate bun
And that is all about me and my owner, Molly.

Molly Hamer (9)
Greenfield St Mary's Primary School, Oldham

The Battle

Screaming and shouting
The soldiers charge,
Across the field
Like a mirage.
The enemy guns crackle and rattle,
The aircraft zoom
Into battle.
They drop their load,
The bombs go *boom!*
Killing hundreds.
They turn around and head back home,
High above the blood and loam.

But from above the men keep running,
Like ants on a patio,
Like waves on a rock,
Like birds in a flock
They hit the rock,
Scrabbling, climbing, falling, dying.

Soon the fields and hills are empty,
Burnt trees and ash,
An eerie cemetery.

James Hall (11)
St Cuthbert's RC Primary School, Walbottle

Black

Black is the soft roof on a car
And a very dark night.
Black is the feeling of sadness,
Or something like a haunted house.
Black is a back alley with nothing in sight.
It's like a cloud indicating a thunderstorm.
It's also the smartest leather on the richest man.
Black is the colour of the coalman's face
And his coal.
It's like the number 8 ball in snooker/pool.
Black is a suit without a single piece of fluff on it.

Ryan Nelson (10)
St Cuthbert's RC Primary School, Walbottle

What Is Red?

Red is an angry bull.
Red is a colour that is not dull.
Red is a scorching flame.
Red is an evil that causes pain.

Red is a corpse pouring with blood,
Red is a creature rolling in the mud.
Red is soft, gentle love,
Red is like a flying dove.

The sound of red is crackle, pop,
Like sausages in a fire from the shop.
Red is the colour of a great ginger cat,
Red is also a baseball bat.

Red is communism.
Red is dark.
Red also colours things in a park.
Imagine a world without red,
Replaced by the same colour as lead.

Alexander Dundon (11)
St Cuthbert's RC Primary School, Walbottle

The Bad Night

Things go bump in the night
To give you a fright
So stay by a light!

As night creeps up on you,
Darkness wraps you in its cloak.
The gale force wind
Feels like ice
Making you shiver.

Things go bump in the night
To give you a fright
So stay by a light!

As you lie in your bed,
Fear gains on you.
The door blows open,
Scratching like a bed of nails
On the blackboard.

Things go bump in the night
To give you a fright
So stay by a light!

Your bed closes in on you
Like a mouth chewing you.
But sleep takes you away
On a boat
Out to sea.

Things go bump in the night
To give you a fright
So stay by a light!

Cameron Hayes (10)
St Cuthbert's RC Primary School, Walbottle

Ghost Rider

A ghostly figure patrols the night,
Giving people an awful fright.
His silhouette glowing in the dark,
That is where he leaves his mark.
He kills one person every dawn
And dumps them on the vicar's lawn.
Oh, he kills in dreadful ways,
It's too bad, too despicable to say.
I lie petrified in my bed,
Stiff as an iceberg it has to be said.
But soon the nightmare will disappear
As I drift to dreamland away from fear.

James Knowles (10)
St Cuthbert's RC Primary School, Walbottle

Ghost Rider

Night is spreading around the world
Darkness has unfurled.
Clip-clopping around the house
Ghost rider has returned.

The wind is howling like a red wolf
In a black space called a gulf.
The door is creaking open like a violin,
So in the covers goes Kilion.

Fear is running down my spine,
Ghost rider is climbing up the vine.
People dying every second,
But sleep is coming to drift you away
To a place where ghost rider doesn't exist.

Courteney Jones (10)
St Cuthbert's RC Primary School, Walbottle

Ghost Rider

What is that slam?

On one Hallowe'en eve,
I hear the whistling of the wind
And the howling of the wolves.
Where am I?
Where do I go?
I don't know,
I don't know!

My nerves are tingling!
My head is sore,
I turned my head,
Who opened the door?
Where am I?
Where do I go?
I don't know,
I don't know!

Is that the ghost rider,
Faint, then loud?
It is the ghost rider,
Trotting tall and proud!
Where am I?
Where do I go?
I don't know,
I don't know!

I don't need to worry now,
Sleep's on its way.
I drift off to a land,
A safe place to stay.

Emma Donaldson (10)
St Cuthbert's RC Primary School, Walbottle

My Ghostly Night

The chilly night blankets the Earth,
A new moon has given birth.
Howling wind like an owl's screech,
The old, gnarled tree is not far from reach.
Darkness clutched the room with its own two fists,
A shadow came forward and suddenly hissed.

Just then the door creaked open like an untuned fiddle,
As the cat leapt on the bed and landed in the middle.
Fear ran down my shivery spine with its own sharp nails.
This night is a horrible story tale.
My trusty bed pulled me in tight,
That night I got such a fright.
I tried to drift off to sleep like a cloud in the sky,
Thank goodness that night I didn't die!

Emily Barnes (10)
St Cuthbert's RC Primary School, Walbottle

Darkness

I wrap up the sky in a great, black blanket,
My friends are the moon and the stars.
I close children's eyes making them sleep.
I am the shadow that looks upon you,
I am your gloomy night.
I am your nightmare under the covers.

Emily Clarke (9)
St Cuthbert's RC Primary School, Walbottle

Fear

I creep about in the dark and scare you!
I am a big, hairy spider on your bedroom wall.
I am noises that make you jump out of your skin!
I creak the floorboards,
I make spooky shadows on your bedroom wall.
I hide behind the garden wall.
The thing that gives you nightmares,
I am fear!

Adam Robson (10)
St Cuthbert's RC Primary School, Walbottle

Silence

Silence is like a ghost town,
With no one around.
It is quiet and it echoes.
I can smell fresh air
And it leaves me with a sweet taste.
I feel relaxed and sleepy
And it reminds me of just me
In my empty room.

Jonathan Mottram (9)
Scholes J&I School, Huddersfield

Anger

It feels like a really hot fire burning you slowly.
It tastes of hot chilli powder getting hotter in your stomach.
It smells of burning bread in the oven.
It sounds like a screaming woman.
It looks like an angry monster all red and burning up.
It reminds me of a forest burning fast.

Maeve Coleman (10)
Scholes J&I School, Huddersfield

Anger

Anger smells like smoke and liquorice.
Anger tastes like a bitter and sour taste.
Anger feels sad and sometimes you feel bad if you did
something wrong.
Anger reminds me of plates crashing and a war.
Anger looks like your mum when she's angry.
Anger sounds like a fast train running past you.

Kieran Valente (9)
Scholes J&I School, Huddersfield

Silence

Silence looks like an empty and deserted place.
It is quiet and it echoes.
It tastes like sour grapes and smells like wallpaper paste
and paint.
It makes me feel really upset and all alone
And reminds me of an open space.

Kirsty Gledhill (9)
Scholes J&I School, Huddersfield

Darkness

Darkness feels like a thousand people trying to kill me.
It puts a bitter taste in my mouth, like cough mixture.
It looks like an endless pit that gets darker and darker as you
look deeper into it.
The pit smells like boiling cabbage in a hot pan that all the water
has gone out of.
It sounds like someone screaming.
Darkness reminds me of death - how someone has lost their life
in an innocent battle.

Elizabeth Powell (9)
Scholes J&I School, Huddersfield

Silence

Silence is like a ghost town with no one around.
It is quiet and it echoes.
I can smell clean, fresh air.
It leaves me with a sweet taste.
I feel relaxed and sleepy,
Reminding me of just me in my empty room.

Connor Radcliffe (9)
Scholes J&I School, Huddersfield

Darkness

Darkness sounds like wolves howling on a dark, wintry night.
It feels like a ghost slowly drifting through me.
Darkness looks like a deserted, pitch-black forest,
Tasting like sour blood running down my throat.
It reminds me of a painful death in a dark, gloomy forest.
Darkness smells like a dead blackbird rotting on the road.

Harriet Kleinman (9)
Scholes J&I School, Huddersfield

Hunger

Hunger feels like you haven't had something to eat
In a long, long time.

Hunger tastes like you really need to have some food
And have a good mumble.

Hunger reminds me of being down in a deep, dark mine.

Hunger sounds like your tummy is going to burst
And your belly rumbles.

Hunger looks like you are really pale
And you look like a zombie.

Hunger smells like a really awful storm
Getting more and more moany.

Amber Francis (9)
Scholes J&I School, Huddersfield

Fun

Fun is like candyfloss dissolving on your red tongue,
The taste of it makes you want more.
It is like looking at your friends, hearing them laugh
And the smiles on their faces.
Fun sounds like music in the distance,
Just listening with your ears to the cool, calm music.
Fun smells like a double cheeseburger with medium fries,
Medium Coke and the smell of the cheese addicts you.
Fun reminds me of a funfair,
You see people just shocked with fun.

Alex Fenwick (9)
Scholes J&I School, Huddersfield

Anger

Anger feels like boiling hot lava inside me and I am about to explode.
It tastes like blood gushing into my mouth.
It smells like rotting - a rotting tree disappearing into oblivion.
It sounds like thousands of people talking to me all at once,
Getting louder and louder and they just won't stop.
It looks like sharks ripping flesh off a human body,
From a person who is still alive.
Anger reminds me of bad times I have had through my life.

Kira O'Brien (10)
Scholes J&I School, Huddersfield

Laughter

Laughter smells like the roses that are given to you
On Valentine's Day.

Laughter feels warm, like when you are asleep in your bed,
All warm and cosy.

Laughter reminds me of that present I always wanted.

Laughter sounds like loud giggles with a side order of sweetness.

Laughter tastes like strawberries wrapped in melted chocolate.

Laughter looks as red as a tomato.

Emily Wade (10)
Scholes J&I School, Huddersfield

Darkness

The reminder of darkness is the good man's grave.
Look round and round to see the dark, dark cave.
All around you hear the flap of the bats,
Then you smell the smell of smoke rising like that.
As something flies past you, feel its leathery wings,
The fiend leaves the taste of its blood drip, dripping.

Alex Jones (10)
Scholes J&I School, Huddersfield

Laughter

Laughter - it looks like a cute, cuddly, furry mammal,
It reminds me of being happy and tastes like the sweetest fruit.
It sounds like the trickle of a beck or the lapping of the ocean
And feels like a sunny day growing in your mind.
It carries the smell of apple pie baking, or grinding coming,
Wherever it goes.

Tom Cousins (9)
Scholes J&I School, Huddersfield

Laughter

Laughter reminds me of falling blossom,
Bursting out of the trees.

Laughter smells like warm cinnamon,
All hot and spicy, but sweet.

Laughter feels warm and welcoming,
Like a bed that's warm in the night.

Laughter sounds like an amusing show,
With dancing and singing and jokes.

Laughter looks like a summer sunset,
With sun blazing across the land.

Laughter tastes like a frothy hot chocolate,
Overflowing with an orange flavour.

Isobel Dewar-Fowler (10)
Scholes J&I School, Huddersfield

Anger

Anger tastes like rotten eggs
And leaves a bitter taste in my mouth.
Anger looks like an empty hole
That goes down and down forever.
It sounds like horrible rock music
And reminds me of a cold, lonely person
Wandering round the streets alone.
It feels like chilli powder getting hotter inside.

Andrew Holmes (9)
Scholes J&I School, Huddersfield

Darkness

Darkness smells like the rotten bones of a dead animal
And tastes like the sourness of the sourest lemon.
It reminds you of blood and guts of a decomposing corpse.
Darkness feels like one thousand knives stabbing into you.
Darkness sounds like one thousand people screaming
and screeching.
Darkness looks like a blazing fire in the dark pit of oblivion.

John Hodgson (9)
Scholes J&I School, Huddersfield

Anger

Anger smells like boiling steam.
It reminds me of a rotting egg.
It sounds like the roaring of an angry lion.
It looks like bubbling lava coming towards me.
It's like I'm on fire and I can't move.
Anger tastes like blood boiling in my mouth.

Jessica Gabbitass (10)
Scholes J&I School, Huddersfield

Anger

Anger sounds like a ferocious dog growling, ready to do its worst.
The feeling is really bad and emotional,
The bitter blood taste is like my heart has burst out, crying with
tears of blood.
Anger is like a big, angry kettle that's going to boil over.
It reminds me of standing on flaming-hot ash and a flaming hot sun.
Anger smells like a poisoned wound, smelling decaying flesh.

Callum Hirst (10)
Scholes J&I School, Huddersfield

Darkness

Darkness feels like death, a rotting corpse.
It looks like a shadowy, pitch-black night,
No one's near, and you're friendless, isolated and solo.
When I think about it in my imagination, it tastes like fresh blood.
It smells like something dying, decaying
And the odour that comes with it is just like a Victorian street.
To me, darkness sounds like people laughing and content,
Then you hear a scream, and all around you, people are rushing
this way and that, panicking.
Darkness reminds me of murder,
When everything and everyone is cheerful, merry, content,
Then you hear something, and that second someone, somewhere
has just died.

Daisy Wilson (10)
Scholes J&I School, Huddersfield

Young Writers Information

We hope you have enjoyed reading this book - and that you will continue to enjoy it in the coming years.

If you like reading and writing poetry drop us a line, or give us a call, and we'll send you a free information pack.

Alternatively if you would like to order further copies of this book or any of our other titles, then please give us a call or log onto our website at www.youngwriters.co.uk

Young Writers Information
Remus House
Coltsfoot Drive
Peterborough
PE2 9JX

(01733) 890066